CIRIA C619

# Sustainable construction award schemes
## – guidance for supply chain leaders

G Chant-Hall

**CIRIA** *sharing knowledge ■ building best practice*

Classic House, 174–180 Old Street, London  EC1V 9BP, UK
TEL   +44 (0)20 7549 3300      FAX   +44 (0)20 7253 0523
EMAIL   enquiries@ciria.org
WEBSITE   www.ciria.org

# Foreword

An award scheme can be very effective in stimulating better practice and innovation, in encouraging people and organisations to perform better, and in bringing those involved in the provision of high quality products and services to the attention of a wide public. This guide is for use by construction clients and main contractors as a framework to assist them develop and run an award scheme based on sustainability criteria for their own suppliers, contractors and designers. The guide will also be of interest to those competing for an award.

*Sustainable construction awards: guidance for supply chain leaders*

Chant-Hall, G

**CIRIA**

C619 © CIRIA 2004 ISBN: 0-86017-619-3

British Library Cataloguing in Publication Data
A catalogue record is available for this book from the British Library.

| Keywords | | |
|---|---|---|
| Sustainable construction, supply chain management, benchmarking and KPIs, project management, environmental good practice, health and safety, sustainable resource use, water quality, pollution prevention, waste minimisation. | | |
| **Reader interest** | **Classification** | |
| Directors | AVAILABILITY | Unrestricted |
| Health and safety managers | CONTENT | Guidance document |
| Environmental managers | | |
| Supply chain and | STATUS | Committee guided |
| procurement managers | | |
| Public relations managers | USER | Directors |
| | | Health and safety managers |
| | | Environmental managers |
| | | Supply chain and |
| | | procurement managers |
| | | Public relations managers |

Published by CIRIA, Classic House, 174-180 Old Street, London EC1V 9BP, UK.

# Acknowledgements

This report is a result of CIRIA research project RP642 Sustainable Construction Client Award Scheme. The project was funded by the DTI through their Partners in Innovation scheme.

CIRIA would like to thank members of the project steering group for their significant contributions throughout the project. The steering group comprised:

| | |
|---|---|
| Gary Thomas (Chair) | Highways Agency |
| John Bowman | Royal Society for the encouragement of Arts, Manufactures and Commerce |
| Edward Eastham | Thames Water Utilities |
| Melanie Grafton | BAA |
| Paul Johnson | Rail Link Engineering |
| John Miller | B&Q |
| David Nowell | BAA Heathrow |
| David Porter | Environment Agency |

*Corresponding members included:*

| | |
|---|---|
| Peter Charnley | The Royal Bank of Scotland Group |
| Simon Fordham | Royal Society for the encouragement of Arts, Manufactures and Commerce |
| Liz McMurtrie | Network Rail |
| Chris Watts | The Housing Corporation |

CIRIA's Project Manager for was Greg Chant-Hall with Owen Jenkins. CIRIA would like to extend particular thanks to all individuals at BAA, Thames Water and Network Rail that were involved in the piloting of award schemes using this guide and also to the RSA for allowing reference to be made to its publication *A Guide to Good Practice: Organising and sponsoring Environment and Sustainable Development Awards*.

# Executive summary

Using previous CIRIA guidance on sustainable construction Key Performance Indicators* as a basis, a framework was developed for construction clients and main contractors to run award schemes based on sustainability for members of their construction supply chain. This framework was then piloted in collaboration with BAA, Thames Water and Network Rail.

There are many benefits to running an award scheme based on sustainable construction. For construction clients and main contractors, such an award scheme provides a mechanism to encourage and recognise best practice, around a range of themes under the banner of sustainability. For supply chain companies such as designers, contractors and materials suppliers, an award scheme provides an excellent opportunity to gain recognition for their contribution to sustainability, from their client and the wider industry.

This report highlights the recommended approach to developing and running an award scheme for construction supply chain companies and includes the case study examples of BAA, Thames Water and Network Rail.

* CIRIA publication *Sustainable construction company indicators* (C563) was published in 2000. The later *Construction industry KPIs*, produced by Construction Best Practice, compliment this guidance.

# Contents

|  |  | Page |
|---|---|---|
| 1 | Introduction to award schemes | 6 |
| | 1.1 Who is the supply chain leader? | |
| | 1.2 Why should you consider an award scheme? | |
| | 1.3 Costs and payback | |
| | 1.4 Types of award schemes | |
| 2 | Introduction to using this guidance | 9 |
| | 2.1 SMEs (Small and Medium sized Enterprises) | |
| | 2.2 Deciding whether to develop a scheme based on environmental or sustainability criteria | |
| | 2.3 Benefits of establishing an award scheme | |
| 3 | Designing an award scheme | 12 |
| | 3.1 Aim of the scheme | |
| | 3.2 Outcome of the scheme | |
| | 3.3 Key participants | |
| | 3.4 The award criteria | |
| | 3.5 Attracting submissions from suppliers and contractors | |
| | 3.6 Award categories | |
| | 3.7 How to select judges | |
| | 3.8 Judging process and assessing supplier performance | |
| | 3.9 Financial issues | |
| | 3.10 Potential sources of funding | |
| | 3.11 Payback and the value of PR and raised profile | |
| | 3.12 Using the exercise as a learning process | |
| | 3.13 Communications strategy | |
| 4 | Awards criteria | 20 |
| | Introduction to sustainability and the Government's principles | |
| | Level 1: Themes | |
| | Level 2: Key issues | |
| | Level 3: Sub issues | |

## Appendices

| | | |
|---|---|---|
| 1 | Award scheme components and suggested annual timeframes | 31 |
| 2 | Matrices to assess supplier performance | 32 |
| 3 | Outline of indicative costs breakdown | 33 |
| 4 | Submission pro forma | 34 |
| 5 | Case studies | 36 |
| 6 | Supporting guidance | 47 |
| 7 | Links to key organisations | 48 |

## References

| | |
|---|---|
| A better quality of life | DETR, 1999 |
| Building a better quality of life | DETR, 2000 |
| Sustainable construction: company indicators (Report C563) | CIRIA, 2001 |
| Social responsibility toolkit for construction clients | CIRIA, (due for publication Autumn 2004) |
| A guide to good practice: Organising and sponsoring environment and sustainable development awards | RSA, 2001 |
| BAA Environmental Awards | BAA, 2000 |
| Thames Water Engineering Awards | Thames Water, 2000 |
| Network Rail Chairman's Environment Awards | Network Rail, 2001 |
| BREEAM – Building Research Establishment Environmental Assessment Methodology | BRE |
| CEEQUAL – Civil Engineering Environmental Quality Assessment and Award Scheme | CEEQUAL Ltd, 2003 |
| BS EN ISO 14001 – Environmental management systems - Specification with guidance for use | International Standards Organisation, 1996 |

## 1

## INTRODUCTION TO AWARD SCHEMES

This guide is based on a study by CIRIA in collaboration with BAA, Thames Water and Network Rail and provides guidance for clients and main contractors who wish to improve the performance of their supply chain through the introduction of a sustainability award scheme. In this guide, sustainability includes consideration of environmental protection and enhancement, social issues and economic growth. However, when developing an award scheme, you can select those criteria of most importance to you and your supply chain.

An award scheme can be very effective in stimulating better practice and innovation, in encouraging people and organisations to perform better, and in bringing those involved in the provision of high quality products and services to the attention of a wide public. This guide is for use by construction clients and main contractors as a framework to assist them develop and run an award scheme for their own suppliers and contractors. The guide may also be of interest to companies submitting entries to an award scheme.

In this guide an award scheme is defined as any scheme that recognises the achievement, in this case criteria to assess achievement is based on sustainability. An award scheme can have just one category and be open to everyone in the supply chain, or alternatively a number of categories can be created to encourage specific entries based on the criteria within each category.

This guide is written in four main sections.

**Section 1** introduces the use of award schemes as a means of improving awareness and encouraging innovation and performance improvement on sustainability issues.

**Section 2** describes this guide, introduces the award scheme criteria and outlines the associated benefits of implementing an award scheme based on this guidance.

**Section 3** details the process of designing and running a successful award scheme, from identifying stakeholders, deciding timeframes, attracting submissions, and arranging the judging and award criteria.

**Section 4** outlines the issues that could be used as possible award criteria, dependant on the on the supply chain leader's objectives, the level of detail within the award scheme could be based on:

- Government principles
- Themes
- Key issues
- Sub issues

Increasing detail, reflecting the importance of the issue to the supply chain leader

Following the main body of this guide, are case studies highlighting the experiences of BAA, Thames Water and Network Rail in establishing award schemes with sustainable construction criteria.

## 1.1 Who is the supply chain leader?

The supply chain leader is likely to be an organisation that is situated fairly high up the construction supply chain, although not necessarily at the top. The supply chain leader may choose to establish an award scheme and this guide has been developed for these organisations. Scheme participants are defined as the suppliers (of either products or services) and contractors/sub-contractors who form the supply chain to these organisations.

| Supply chain leaders | A client organisation that procures construction | A main contractor |
|---|---|---|

award scheme for ...

| Supply chain participants | ○ suppliers of either services or products<br>○ main contractors<br>○ sub-contractors | ○ suppliers of either services or products<br>○ sub-contractors |
|---|---|---|

Please note that where supply chain participants could be main contractors or sub-contractors, they have been referred to as "contractors" throughout this guide.

## 1.2    Why should you consider an award scheme?

○ Do you wish to raise awareness of sustainability issues throughout your company or supply chain?

○ Are you looking for more effective ways of promoting your sustainability policies and aims to your supply chain?

○ Do you aim to stimulate the adoption of good sustainability best practice through your supply chain?

○ Could you benefit from a mechanism that encourages your supply chain companies and your own organisation to learn from each other?

○ Are you interested in encouraging sustainability best practice as a means of delivering a better service?

○ Do you wish to reward suppliers and contractors for helping you to achieve your sustainability aspirations?

○ Are you interested in increased internal networking and team building?

○ Do you want to put sustainability onto the business agenda, highlighting the business case to your staff and stakeholders?

Developing an award scheme for your supply chain may help you to achieve or facilitate some of the above aims.

## 1.3    Costs and payback

Developing an award scheme will have associated costs, both in money and time. Based on experience, CIRIA estimates that, including staff time and external costs, an award scheme could be developed for between £11 000 and £50 000. Cost is dependant on the scope of the award scheme but this range has been based on CIRIA's work with BAA plc, who in 2000 established an extremely successful environmental award scheme for its supply chain, Thames Water Utilities and Network Rail (see Appendix 5). The payback on initial investment may come through increased supply-chain partnering and reduced tender costs in the future. There are also a number of other factors that have an economic perspective, including:

○ **publicity and public relations:** positive press releases, radio, and television features

○ **social:** improving relationships with stakeholders including suppliers, contractors, local community, and Non Government Organisations (NGOs) such as Greenpeace, the New Economics Foundation, Forum for the Future, and the World Wildlife Foundation

○ **environmental:** positively managing the supply chain's impact on the environment, for example minimising resource use, waste creation and pollution.

Although some of the above benefits are less tangible there can be little doubt that they benefit and add value to the organisation concerned.

## 1.4 Types of award scheme

Award schemes can operate at an international, national, regional, professional, market, topic, or product level. Companies submitting applications through each of these award schemes will have differing aims, some of which are outlined below. The receipt of an award can instil a tremendous pride in the individual, the team and the organisation by being acknowledged as the best in the field.

| TYPE | AIM |
| --- | --- |
| Individual/team award: | Recognition and acknowledgement for the individual/team and the organisation or cause they serve. |
| Building award: | Recognition and acknowledgement for the team, setting a benchmark for industry. |
| Product/service award: | Recognition and acknowledgement for the organisation. Marketing advantage, increasing confidence of customers. |
| Sustainability reporting award: | Recognition and acknowledgement for the organisation. Marketing advantage, increasing confidence of customers, investors and other stakeholders. |
| Business excellence award: | Recognition and acknowledgement for the organisation. Increasing confidence of customers, investors and other stakeholders. |

Depending on your aims as a supply chain leader and the aims of your supply chain, you may choose to take a particular focus for your award scheme, which could be based on some of those above.

## 2

## INTRODUCTION TO USING THIS GUIDE

In addition to the above, award schemes can also be used within companies or in a construction context, within supply chains.

The CIRIA study was not about creating another national award scheme. The purpose was to provide guidance for supply chain leaders who wish to improve the sustainability performance of their supply chain through the introduction of their own award scheme. This guide includes specific criteria that can be used to gauge the performance of supply chain members.

By giving each of the criteria an importance weighting, each supply chain leader is able to establish a bespoke scheme, ensuring it is suited to their supply chain and tailored to individual requirements and objectives.

A well-designed award scheme will achieve some, if not all, of the following:

○ recognition of an individual's or a team's efforts by peers, industry, suppliers and customers

○ celebrating an achievement of a group, process or a product

○ sharing knowledge and lessons learned through experience

○ a means of informal benchmarking

○ engendering a spirit of cooperation and positive competition

○ encouraging the use of new approaches

○ motivation of individuals, teams and supply chain organisations to continually improve practices.

This approach ensures those not involved in high profile national or international schemes are also recognised for their achievement, commitment and contribution to the success of their company.

This report considers how schemes can be introduced within companies or supply chains with the primary aim of encouraging and recognising good sustainability performance. Many of the principles will also apply to other endeavours, innovations, business process improvement schemes, or product awards.

This guide can be used by different supply chain leaders to establish a wide range of award schemes. The guidance is relevant for a scheme which relates to the construction process and also for a scheme which relates to the end product, ie a building or infrastructure. The framework outlined can be adopted to run a range of different award schemes, whether individual, focused on certain criteria or based on particular categories. See sections 3.4 and 4 for further details.

## 2.1    SMEs (small and medium-sized enterprises)

Any company with fewer than 250 employees and with an annual turnover not exceeding £50 million is classed as an SME. Such companies can make a significant contribution to more sustainable construction. The resources, market and priorities of these businesses are, however, different from those of larger consultancy and contracting companies.

Participation in an award scheme, led by a supply chain leader, is nevertheless relevant to SMEs because they also will be able to improve their sustainability performance through improved information, training and awareness, and via the sub-contracting system. In some ways many SMEs take a lead undertaking a sustainable approach, particularly with reference to a locally-based workforce, local links and training. It is also worth noting that SMEs have a greater degree of flexibility to adapt quickly to change, in a way that larger organisations find difficult to match.

## 2.2 Deciding whether to develop a scheme based on environmental or sustainability criteria

Sustainable construction is recognised as having three strands: environmental, social and economic:

○ environmentally the industry consumes more than 200 million tonnes of primary aggregate, produces over 70 million tonnes of waste and is responsible for in excess of 500 water pollution incidents each year

○ economically the industry has an annual turnover of over £50 billion (more than 10 per cent of GDP) and employs well over a million people

○ socially the industry is important, both in terms of delivering the buildings and infrastructure needed to maintain our standard of living, and its influence on sustainable communities, as described in the DETR sustainable development strategy *A better quality of life*.

The economic strand has always been important to the construction industry, however profit margins still tend to be relatively low when compared with other industries. The construction industry's massive £50 billion turnover gives huge scope for better management, improved sustainability performance and cost savings, which will lead to an improved bottom line. The majority of the construction industry is still coming to terms with the relationship between economic factors and either environmental or social issues, although some companies are making good progress towards sustainability as a whole.

If you feel that your organisation's current focus is primarily on one of these issues, for example environmental issues, then this report will still help you consider whether an award scheme will support your aims of improving your performance.

## 2.3 Benefits of establishing an award scheme

The development and implementation of an award scheme provides many advantages to all involved in the process. The precise nature of these benefits is dependant on the specification of the individual supply chain leader's scheme. An indicative summary of the benefits that may be achieved is shown opposite:

| Benefits for supply chain leaders: | Benefits for supply chain participants: |
|---|---|
| ○ Highlights opportunities for improvement and cost savings through the tender and project process | ○ Builds on existing relationships with supply chain leaders and other companies |
| ○ Highlights potential environmental, social and economic risks resulting from supply chain activities | ○ Recognition from supply chain leader, public and other stakeholders |
| | ○ Gains visibility for the organisation and its products or services |
| ○ Builds on existing relationships with supply chain companies | ○ Increases knowledge of other supply chain companies' operations |
| ○ Increases knowledge of supply chain companies' operations | ○ Increase of market share |
| | ○ Improves employee performance and morale |
| ○ Uses measurement and assessment of supply chain companies to benchmark the performance of supply chain companies | ○ Highlights opportunities for improvement and cost savings |
| | ○ Gain understanding of the sustainability objectives and challenges within their own company |
| | ○ Highlights potential environmental, social and economic risks and challenges |
| ○ Increases the likelihood and ease with which a supply chain company could report on any aspect of performance (environmental, social or economic) | ○ Provides a stimulus for focusing projects towards sustainable construction, promoting the implementation of better practice within the company. This may lead to more efficient and competitive company processes and the construction of more sustainable assets |
| ○ Recognition from stakeholders, including shareholders and investors | ○ Provides quantitative data to enable analysis of past performance, and enhance learning from these experiences |
| ○ Helps align the supply chain towards a common sustainability policy. | ○ Facilitates development of monitoring mechanisms, against which to measure progress |
| | ○ Benchmarks performance against competitors within the same supply chain (and possibly beyond) |
| **Benefits to wider stakeholders:** | ○ Increases the likelihood and ease of reporting company performance against the criteria set by the supply chain leader, on any aspect of performance (environmental, social or economic). In turn this may lead to: |
| ○ Encourages other supply chain leaders to adopt award schemes for sustainable construction. | ○ demonstrating to regulators and Government that the company is complying with requirements and is at the forefront of initiatives to improve performance in helping to build effective working relationships |
| ○ Encourages benchmarking between supply chains | ○ demonstrating that the company is responding to supply chain leaders' concerns and needs |
| ○ Builds confidence in quality of performance and compliance. | ○ encouraging employees to apply good practice and add urgency to the need for change |
| | ○ facilitating dialogue with stakeholder groups |
| | ○ building the trust of the local community and neighbours, making subsequent expansion or changes to operating practices easier to achieve |
| | ○ informing the wider community through the company's own words and actions and not those of journalists and pressure groups that may misrepresent the company |
| | ○ demonstrating to the supply chain leader and other stakeholders such as clients, lenders, investors, insurers and others, that the business is well-managed and is seeking to reduce risks and minimise future liabilities. |

## DESIGNING AN AWARD SCHEME

### 3.1    Aim of the scheme

Introducing an award scheme to improve awareness and encourage innovation and performance improvement is similar to introducing any business improvement initiative and requires a similar degree of planning. Many well-intentioned initiatives fail to achieve their potential because a number of factors were not considered at the planning stages. In the context of an award scheme for the supply-chain, these are:

○    clear understanding of your own sustainability challenges

○    what is the aim or desired outcome of the scheme?

○    who are the key participants?

### 3.2    Outcome of the scheme

Section 2 listed a range of possible benefits of award schemes. It is unlikely that all these benefits will be valued equally by all supply chain leaders. For organisations with established teams and supply chains, the focus might be on improving measurable performance, linking to construction industry Key Performance Indicators (KPIs). For organisations with newer supply chains, the priority might be to encourage knowledge sharing etc. If an award scheme is to compete with other potential internal initiatives, then clear potential benefits need to be identified at the earliest opportunity. In many instances, these can support other company initiatives spanning not only the key themes of sustainability, but also wider initiatives such as training, and communication.

### 3.3    Key participants

The prestige associated with national award schemes and the funding available to promoters in terms of advertising and PR are often sufficient alone to encourage submissions by participants. The introduction of an internal scheme requires a number of factors to be considered:

○    the cost of developing and running the scheme

○    the material that individuals or teams will be expected to submit

○    who the beneficiaries will be (this may be wider than the supply chain)

○    whether participants are likely to require approval to participate from within their organisation, and if so, from whom

○    identifying who should be involved in the development of the scheme. This includes the design, consultation, setting criteria, judges and others, in addition to those who need to be aware of the existence of the scheme at a more general level.

An award scheme based on sustainability will, by definition, span a number of areas within the company, including health and safety and HR, finance, procurement, external relations and facilities management. The scheme will, clearly, require wider consultation than an environmental scheme, which might be promoted only by the organisation's environmental management group or contracts department.

It is also worth identifying a point in the development of the scheme for formal approval. The agreement of Aims (3.1), Outcomes (3.2), and Criteria (3.4) forms such a point. A brief document setting these out will form a clear point of reference during the subsequent development stages and a starting point for discussions with judges. Finally, it is worth considering early on in the process whether, in developing the scheme, you wish to work alongside a consultant or other independent advisor.

Considering these factors early on and engaging the relevant stakeholders should help to both raise awareness of the scheme and improve its take-up. Details of the awards criteria are shown on the flow diagram below. Suggested timeframes for each component (on an annual basis) are shown in Appendix 1.

## Starting point

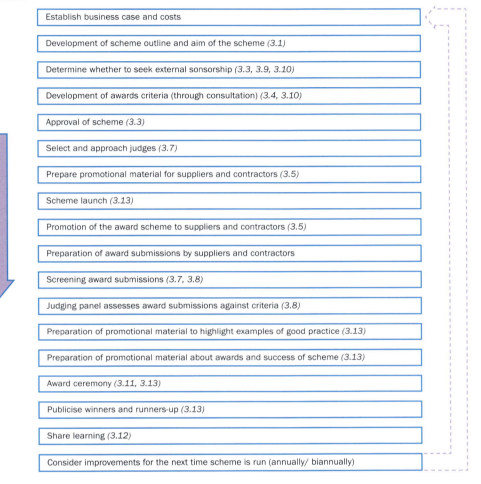

## 3.4 The awards criteria: Linking your priorities with the most suitable award scheme for you

Since an award scheme is about raising awareness and improving performance, the categories and criteria adopted, and the shape of the scheme itself, will depend on:

- where you consider your organisation/supply chain to be in terms of its present sustainability performance and

- your aims for the organisation in terms of level of performance and rate of change.

If you are seeking external sponsorship, the objectives of the sponsor will also need to be considered.

> For example, looking at environmental issues... at one extreme you may consider that your organisation has not really embraced environmental issues and that certain parts of your supply chain may be struggling with environmental compliance. The award scheme may be required to help to promote the basic message of "environmental sense is business sense". At the other, you may have clearly-defined environmental targets and be expecting your suppliers to perform beyond minimum regulatory requirements. The award scheme may be required to demonstrate how performance standards are being raised, and the processes by which this is being achieved. Most companies will fall between these two extremes, or be attaining different levels of performance for different issues.

You will also need to consider whether you are promoting the scheme as a sustainable construction scheme or whether you plan to focus on one or two of the sustainability strands, ie environmental, social and economic.

The awards criteria cover all issues related to sustainable construction (see Section 4 which describes each of the criteria in detail). These criteria are split into three levels, which correspond to how relevant and important you consider each criteria to be. The different levels outline how you assess the performance of your supply chain. To illustrate how this works, the example of "avoiding pollution" has been included.

Setting award criteria

Implementation to achieve more sustainable construction

| Overarching objective | Government principle | Theme | Key issues | Sub-issues |
|---|---|---|---|---|
| | | Level 1 | Level 2 | Level 3 |
| | | Medium importance (to supply chain leader) | High importance (to supply chain leader) | Very High importance (to supply chain leader) |
| Sustainability | Is the associated Government principle related to environmental, social or economic performance? | This level examines the *themes* of the area. At this level, assessment of supply-chain performance is generic and qualitative. Supply chain companies are assessed on whether they are taking any action (the specific actions that they may be taking are not examined in great detail) | This level examines the *key issues* within each of the key themes. This level of assessment is primarily qualitative, drawing on quantitative assessment where relevant. | This level examines the *sub issues* within each of the significant issues. At this level, assessment is primarily quantitative, using qualitative assessment as a preliminary mechanism. Supply chain companies are assessed on the detailed action they are taking and the measurement and supporting records they can provide (where practicable) to demonstrate their performance. |
| Sustainability | Effective protection of the environment and prudent use of natural resources | Avoiding pollution | Measures implemented to avoid mitigate and manage pollution from site | Has an EMS been implemented? (documented appraisal of significant impacts, documented objectives and targets for improved performance) |
| | | | | Is the EMS formally accredited to recognised standard? (eg ISO 14001 or EMAS). |
| | | | | Identification of potential pollution sources and design of mitigation measures |
| | | | | Minimising polluting emissions on site |
| | | | | Effective site supervision (where consultant is employed in a client resident engineer capacity). |
| | | | | Preventing nuisance from noise and dust by good site management |
| | | | | Preventing pollution incidents and breaches of environmental legislative requirements. |

## 3.5 Attracting submissions from suppliers and contractors

An award scheme's success is attributable partly to the number and quality of the entries received, from which outstanding winners can be selected. There are several mechanisms that supply chain leaders can use to ensure that submissions from suppliers and contractors are attracted. Solutions are focused in two areas: firstly making the entry process simple and secondly, finding better incentives and recognition for organisations that participate, not just those that win. Each supply chain leader will choose which of these to use for their own scheme. A major disincentive to entering award schemes is the need for long and complex submissions. This is a particular hurdle for SMEs. Members of the supply chain could be encouraged to enter the scheme by a combination of the following:

- nomination
- invitation
- advertisement, or
- publicity – public relations.

Publicity material should be clear and should include the criteria that the judges will be looking for. A simple statement of the aims of the exercise and a statement of endorsement from a senior board member will also demonstrate commitment to the scheme.

## 3.6 Awards categories

There are a number of ways that you may wish to develop your award scheme. You may wish to have an open competition and only one winner. Alternatively, and at the other end of the spectrum, you may wish to develop a number of awards categories, offering first, second and third places in each. Categories can be based on type or organisation, type of issue or the nature of the innovation. Below are some ideas that you may wish to consider:

- business units within your own organisation
- innovative design
- large contractors
- smaller contractors
- awards focused on particular criteria, for example best contractor in the field of waste management, or contribution to biodiversity
- special category: which could be for most innovative project/contractor for example.

However you develop your awards categories it is important to highlight that there are no losers in your award scheme and that all entries are given recognition of their contribution to sustainable construction within your supply chain.

Given the uncertainties surrounding the first time of running a scheme, there may be an advantage in maintaining a flexibility over award categories until after initial submissions are entered.

## 3.7 How to select judges

The selection of the right judges is key to the success of your award scheme. Judges need to be well versed in the construction process and sustainability issues, and highly committed to the success of your scheme. These skills will enable judges to assess and compare the merits of very different applications. The better recognised that these experts are, the more credible your awards will be. It is an advantage if some or all of the judges are seen to be independent of the organisation.

It is recommended that in order to highlight the commitment to your award scheme, any judges that are internal to your organisation should be from high level management.

Judges can provide an award scheme with a great deal of recognition and credibility. For example, consider inviting representatives from the following organisations to sit on your judging panel:

- NGOs such as Friends of the Earth, Greenpeace, and the World Wildlife Foundation

- charitable organisations working in the fields of environment and sustainability such as Business in the Community and Forum for the Future.

- government representatives at central or regional level, such as government offices and regional development agencies.

- research organisations

- other companies from within the construction industry (perhaps offering your skills to appraise their award scheme in return)

- trades associations and other industry bodies recognised by the supply chain and other stakeholders.

Many of the above are not-for-profit or charitable organisations. If you choose to invite judges from these organisations you may find that they require payment. Ensure that your scheme has the budget to facilitate this and agree the time required and fees in advance, (see Appendix 3 and Appendix 7).

It is beneficial to use judges that are complimentary (ie from differing backgrounds as detailed above), as this is likely to propagate interesting discussions and will ensure that submissions are appraised with as wide a perspective as possible. There will be a distinct advantage in involving your judges in the appraisal stage of the award scheme process.

## 3.8    Judging process and assessing supplier performance

**The judging process can be flexible; from a subjective level to a very rigorous objective level, dependant on the supply chain leader's priorities and requirements.**

Overarching objective of sustainability

Government principles

| | | |
|---|---|---|
| 1 | Themes | generic, subjectively appraised |
| 2 | Key- issues | intermediate appraisal |
| 3 | Sub-issues | quantitative appraisal examining measured outputs. |

When assessing the performance of suppliers and contractors against each criteria, your level of requirement, (Level 1, 2 or 3), is of key importance as this provides an indication of how well you expect suppliers and contractors to perform. As the level of importance increases, so the stringent nature of assessment increases. For example, at a Level 3 assessment for any given criteria, you may wish to consider the following points:

- does the company ensure its performance is monitored?

- how is performance monitored? (eg periodic audits)

- does the company keep records that could provide evidence of performance?

- can the company quantify its performance? (eg percentage waste recycled/number of near misses)

- does the company use indicators to assess its performance in this area?

The assessment process will usually be desk based, but site visits to check some of the criteria may be appropriate for some schemes.

At a general level the judging criteria should cover some of the following aspects:

- quality of submission/application
- degree of originality/innovation
- the relevance of the subject entry
- evidence of substantive measurable impact and or benefits (environmental, economic or social)
- demonstrable programme for promotion and dissemination of work
- level of involvement of relevant stakeholders
- continual improvement and sustainability of approach
- transferability within your business/supply chain.

Specific judging criteria for the supplier assessment process are detailed in Section 4.

A clear set of tasks and principles will need to be agreed with judges. These will include:

- whether judges are involved in the short-listing process
- whether communication between judges will be at arranged judges' meetings
- whether judges are expected to consult other judges at other times.

Even if the criteria are subjective, it is always preferable to have some form of pro forma for use by the judges. While such forms cannot be relied upon to yield a clear set of winners, they are a valuable way of identifying and debating differences in views across the judging panel. See Appendix 2.

## 3.9    Financial issues

The cost of establishing an award scheme will vary depending on the scope of each supply chain leader's scheme, and whether in-house staff have the requisite skills to develop a scheme without buying in expert advice. Indicative figures based on CIRIA's research are that an effective award scheme could be set up with minimal external costs. Even allowing for staff time at £200 per day, an effective scheme could be established for as little as £11 000 and a comprehensive and highly prestigious scheme could be set up for around £50 000. CIRIA recommends that an award scheme uses efficiencies wherever possible and that components with an additional cost are only factored in where significant value is added. Using this approach would cost approximately £25 000. A full breakdown of the differences between each end of the spectrum is shown in Appendix 3.

The least expensive means of scheme development ties in closely with existing activities, which greatly reduces the cost of running the award scheme. To assist with the cost of the scheme it may be appropriate for some supply chain leaders to consider attracting sponsors. Likely sponsors will be dependant on the type of work undertaken by the supply chain leader and their contacts with potential sponsorship organisations.

## 3.10 Potential sources of funding

It may be suitable for supply chain leaders to approach the following organisations regarding funding or part-funding of their award scheme:

- DTI
- DEFRA
- Regional Development Agencies
- Local Government Offices
- other organisations offering local business support may also be able to help.

External sponsors are likely to want input into the development of the award scheme. If this is possible it should be brought to the attention of such organisations as it may encourage more sponsorship.

## 3.11 Payback and the value of PR and raised profile

The payback on the initial investment made by the construction supply chain leader will come in several ways, which may be directly economic through increased partnering approaches with awards participants and reduced tender costs for all parties. Other economic benefits may be cost savings made through the project process linked to increased communication of all parties. In addition to these economic benefits will come further benefits which may be less tangible but of no less value. These may include increased PR, and an increase of perceived stakeholder value. These and similar factors are likely to show their value over the longer timeframe in the way of increased market share and increased turnover and profitability. Establishing an award scheme for sustainable construction may also act as a form of insurance against receiving negative publicity.

## 3.12 Using the exercise as a learning process

While the focus of such a scheme will be driven by the final award date, there may be opportunities to share the learning between participants. One way of doing this would be to invite short-listed candidates to make a brief presentation in front of other supply chain members. This need not necessarily coincide with the award presentation. There may be benefit for senior representatives from your own company to attend these presentations, to learn what has been done and the benefits achieved.

## 3.13 Communication strategy

A communication strategy should be drawn up as soon as possible to identify key stages, messages and target audiences. These might include:

- announcement of the scheme and launch details
- announcement of the number of submissions
- highlighting examples of good practice included in submissions
- brief synopsis of the short-listed submissions
- in-depth analysis of the winning submissions with clear illustration of why they won, the benefits delivered and the learning opportunities created.

# 4    AWARDS CRITERIA

Section 3.4 described how you can establish the basic scope and how to start focusing on specific criteria. This section provides additional information to help you through the detail of this process. The awards criteria displayed on the forthcoming pages are based on indicators developed by CIRIA in report *Sustainable construction: company indicators* C563. In addition, you may wish to refer to schemes such as BREEAM and CEEQUAL.

The awards criteria increase in detail from Level 1 to Level 3. The Key Themes (Level 1) are based on Government and industry documents. The Significant Issues (Level 2) and Specific Components (Level 3) are based on a number of sources (including CIRIA publication C563) produced in collaboration with the industry in 2001.

The level on which the award criteria is based will be dependant on how important and how relevant each of the criteria are to the organisation and its supply chain. These can also be seen on the supplier performance assessment matrix in Appendix 2.

The overarching objective of an award scheme is to improve the sustainability performance of companies in the supply chain.

In 2000 the Government published *Building a better quality of life – a strategy for sustainable development for the United Kingdom*. This document stated the government's principles for sustainable development to improve performance environmentally, socially and economically. Specifically:

- effective protection of the environment
- social progress which recognises the needs of everyone
- maintenance of high and sustainable levels of economic growth, employment and profitability

To help construction companies to achieve improvements against each of the government principles above, CIRIA developed and produced *Sustainable construction: company indicators* which put forward 12 themes, that underpin each of the government principles.

| Government Principle | Theme (Level 1) |
|---|---|
| Effective protection of the environment and prudent use of natural resources | Avoiding pollution |
| | Protecting and enhancing biodiversity |
| | Improving energy efficiency and management |
| | Efficient use of resources |
| | Transport and travel planning |
| Social progress which recognises the needs of everyone | Respect for people |
| | Working with local communities |
| | Partnership working |
| Maintenance of high and stable levels of economic growth and employment | Sustained and increased productivity and profitability |
| | Improved project delivery |
| | Monitoring and reporting performance against targets |
| | Designing for whole life costing (life cycle analysis) |

When developing a sustainable construction award scheme, other important factors should also be considered as possible criteria. These cut across the government's environmental, social and economic principles. These **cross-principle issues** are:

- ○ Influence over competitors and other manufacturers
- ○ Technology transfer
- ○ Innovation
- ○ Learning

In turn, each of the themes outlined above are underpinned by series of key issues, which in turn are supported by a series of sub-issues. Further details and the relationships between these issues and the themes, government principles and overarching objectives are shown on the following pages.

| Overarching Objective | Government principles | Theme for Award Scheme<br><br>Level 1 | Key issues for Award Scheme criteria<br><br>Level 2 | Sub-issues for Award Scheme criteria<br><br>Level 3 | Applicable to (design/ construction/generic) |
|---|---|---|---|---|---|
| Sustainability | Effective protection of the environment | Avoiding pollution | Measures implemented to avoid, mitigate and manage pollution from site | Has an EMS been implemented? (documented appraisal of significant impacts, documented objectives and targets for improved performance) | g |
| | | | | Is the EMS formally accredited to recognised standard? (eg ISO 14001 or EMAS). | g |
| | | | | Identification of potential pollution sources and design of mitigation measures | d |
| | | | | Minimising polluting emissions on site | c |
| | | | | Effective site supervision (where consultant is employed in a client resident engineer capacity). | d |
| | | | | Preventing nuisance from noise and dust by good site management | c |
| | | | | Preventing pollution incidents and breaches of environmental legislative requirements | c |

| Overarching Objective | Government principles | Theme for Award Scheme<br><br>Level 1 | Key issues for Award Scheme criteria<br><br>Level 2 | Sub-issues for Award Scheme criteria<br><br>Level 3 | Applicable to (design/construction/generic) |
|---|---|---|---|---|---|
| Sustainability | Effective protection of the environment | Avoiding pollution and efficient use of resources | Transport planning | Greening fleet of company cars | g |
| | | | | Route planning | g |
| | | | | Car sharing | g |
| | | | | Percentage of public transport use for company business | g |
| | | | | Percentage of no-emission travel (cycling etc) | g |
| | | | | Development of green commuting plan | g |
| | | | | Minimising travel | g |
| Sustainability | Effective protection of the environment | Protecting and enhancing biodiversity | Protecting existing species and enhancing biodiversity | Protecting sensitive ecosystems through good design practices | g |
| Sustainability | Effective protection of the environment | Protecting and enhancing biodiversity | Habitat creation and environmental improvement | Has an environmental appraisal been undertaken and environmental mitigation measures implemented? | g |
| | | | | Identification of opportunities to enhance biodiversity by habitat creation | d |
| | | | | Design-in environmental improvements such as by landscaping or habitat creation | d |
| | | | | Specification of native species for planting/seeding | d |
| | | | | Protecting sensitive ecosystems through good design practices. | d |
| | | | | Planting of native species | c |
| | | | | Protecting sensitive ecosystems through good construction practices and supervision | c |
| | | | | Dealing with unforeseen protected/ harmful species | c |

| Overarching Objective | Government principles | Theme for Award Scheme Level 1 | Key issues for Award Scheme criteria Level 2 | Sub-issues for Award Scheme criteria Level 3 | Applicable to (design/ construction/generic) |
|---|---|---|---|---|---|
| Sustainability | Effective protection of the environment | Protecting and enhancing biodiversity | Optimising use of brownfield sites | Utilising brownfield sites in favour of greenfield sites | d |
| Sustainability | Effective protection of the environment | Protecting and enhancing biodiversity | Environmentally sensitive design and construction | Consideration of flora and fauna, landscape | g |
| Sustainability | Effective protection of the environment | Improving energy efficiency and management | Designing for whole life costs | Energy efficient building design | d |
| | | | | Energy efficient construction processes | c |
| | | | | Reduced energy consumption in business activities | g |
| Sustainability | Effective protection of the environment | Improving energy efficiency and management | Use of local supplies and materials with low embodied energy | Incorporation of renewable energy sources or combined heat and power schemes into development design | d |
| Sustainability | Effective protection of the environment | Improved energy efficiency | Better management of existing facilities | | g |
| Sustainability | Effective protection of the environment | Improved energy efficiency | Use of renewable energy sources | | g |
| Sustainability | Effective protection of the environment | Efficient use of resources | Waste minimisation and managemenrt | Propose lean designs avoiding over-engineering | d |
| | | | | Design for whole-life costs and minimum waste in construction, use and afterlife | d |
| | | | | Lean construction avoiding waste | c |
| | | | | Waste management plan implemented | c |
| | | | | Reusing materials, including those already on site (where applicable through treatment) | c |
| | | | | Use recycled/reclaimed materials, or those from sustainable supplies or with low embodied energies | c |
| | | | | Conserve water during construction | c |

| Overarching Objective | Government principles | Theme for Award Scheme Level 1 | Key issues for Award Scheme criteria Level 2 | Sub-issues for Award Scheme criteria Level 3 | Applicable to (design/ construction/generic) |
|---|---|---|---|---|---|
| Sustainability | Effective protection of the environment | Efficient use of resources | Reuse of existing built assets | Specify reclaimed/recycled materials | d |
| | | | | Specifiy materials from sustainable supplies | d |
| | | | | Specify materials with low embodied energies | d |
| Sustainability | Effective protection of the environment | Efficient use of resources | Use of reclaimed/recycled/ sustainably-sourced products | Use of reclaimed/recycled materials | c |
| | | | | Use of materials from sustainable supplies | c |
| | | | | Use of materials with low embodied energies | c |
| Sustainability | Effective protection of the environment | Efficient use of resources | Lean design and construction | Designing and constructing using materials efficiently and effectively | g |
| Sustainability | Effective protection of the environment | Efficient use of resources | Water conservation | Design to conserve water in use including, where appropriate, rainfall capture and greywater systems | d |
| | | | | Conserve water during construction | c |
| Sustainability | Social progress which recognises the needs of everyone | Respect for people | Provision of effective training and appraisals | Commitment – to invest in people to achieve business goals | g |
| | | | | Planning – how skills, individuals and teams are to be developed to achieve these goals | g |
| | | | | Taking action – to develop and use necessary skills in a well defined and continuing programme directly tied to business objectives | g |
| | | | | Evaluating – outcomes of training and development for individuals' progress towards goals, the value achieved and future needs | g |
| | | | | Reportable fatal and non-fatal accidents | g |

| Overarching Objective | Government principles | Theme for Award Scheme<br><br>Level 1 | Key issues for Award Scheme criteria<br><br>Level 2 | Sub-issues for Award Scheme criteria<br><br>Level 3 | Applicable to (design/construction/generic) |
|---|---|---|---|---|---|
| Sustainability | Social progress which recognises the needs of everyone | Respect for people | Building effective channels of communication | Projects that include (and implement) a plan to consult with the end user | g |
| Sustainability | Social progress which recognises the needs of everyone | Respect for people | Equitable terms and conditions | Partnership working (building long-term relationships with supply chain leaders, building long-term relationships with suppliers) | g |
| | | | | Pay rates comparable with industry averages | g |
| | | | | Company benefits applicable to all staff, (ie subsidised fares, private health insurance) | g |
| Sustainability | Social progress which recognises the needs of everyone | Respect for people | Provision of equal opportunities | Provision of a conducive working environment for all | g |
| Sustainability | Social progress which recognises the needs of everyone | Respect for people | Health, safety and provision of a conducive working environment | Refer CIRIA report C627 *Social responsibility toolkit for construction clients* | g |
| Sustainability | Social progress which recognises the needs of everyone | Respect for people | Maintaining morale and employee satisfaction | Refer CIRIA report C627 *Social responsibility toolkit for construction clients* | g |
| Sustainability | Social progress which recognises the needs of everyone | Respect for people | Participation in decision-making | Refer CIRIA report C627 *Social responsibility toolkit for construction clients* | g |
| Sustainability | Social progress which recognises the needs of everyone | Respect for people | Ensuring legal employment practices | All members of staff insured and part of National Insurance scheme. | g |
| Sustainability | Social progress which recognises the needs of everyone | Respect for people | Ethical investment regarding development of own organisation | Refer CIRIA report C627 *Social responsibility toolkit for construction clients* | g |
| Sustainability | Social progress which recognises the needs of everyone | Respect for people | Ethical investment regarding other companies | Refer CIRIA report C627 *Social responsibility toolkit for construction clients* | g |

| Overarching Objective | Government principles<br><br>Level 1 | Theme for Award Scheme<br><br>Level 1 | Key issues for Award Scheme criteria<br><br>Level 2 | Sub-issues for Award Scheme criteria<br><br>Level 3 | Applicable to (design/ construction/generic) |
|---|---|---|---|---|---|
| Sustainability | Social progress which recognises the needs of everyone | Working with local communities | Minimising local nuisance (eg noise, vibration, dust, odour, light) | Number of formal environmental or nuisance notices served due to construction activities (affecting or arising from habitat or biodiversity, air quality emissions or dust, noise, waste disposal, spillage to water, river damage, land contamination, damage to heritage, access rights) | g |
| | | | | Considerate Contractors Scheme (considerate, environmentally aware, clean, a good neighbour, respectful, safe, responsible, accountable) | g |
| Sustainability | Social progress which recognises the needs of everyone | Working with local communities | Minimising local nuisance (eg congestion) | Refer CIRIA report C627 *Social responsibility toolkit for construction clients* | g |
| Sustainability | Social progress which recognises the needs of everyone | Working with local communities | Building effective channels of communication | Appropriate projects that include (and implement) a plan for stakeholder dialogue, | g |
| Sustainability | Social progress which recognises the needs of everyone | Working with local communities | Contributing to the local economy/ providing local employment | Refer CIRIA report C627 *Social responsibility toolkit for construction clients* | g |
| Sustainability | Social progress which recognises the needs of everyone | Working with local communities | Delivering products and services that enhance the local environment | Refer CIRIA report C627 *Social responsibility toolkit for construction clients* | g |
| Sustainability | Social progress which recognises the needs of everyone | Working with local communities | Education: within schools and community groups | Refer CIRIA report C627 *Social responsibility toolkit for construction clients* | g |
| Sustainability | Social progress which recognises the needs of everyone | Working with local communities | Social inclusion | Refer CIRIA report C627 *Social responsibility toolkit for construction clients* | g |
| Sustainability | Social progress which recognises the needs of everyone | Working with local communities | Involving communities in the decision making process | To what degree standards of environmental performance and social engagement have been formally agreed with the client, eg the energy efficiency of the structure (beyond minimum building standards), the need for and choice of heating and cooling systems, opportunities to use prefabricated materials or those with low embodied energy, use of secondary materials, landscaping or habitat creation opportunities, environmental performance of contractors (such as the need to have an EMS) | g |

| Overarching Objective | Government principles | Theme for Award Scheme<br><br>Level 1 | Key issues for Award Scheme criteria<br><br>Level 2 | Sub-issues for Award Scheme criteria<br><br>Level 3 | Applicable to (design/construction/generic) |
|---|---|---|---|---|---|
| Sustainability | Social progress which recognises the needs of everyone | Partnership working | Building long-term relationships with clients | Refer CIRIA report C627 *Social responsibility toolkit for construction clients* | g |
| Sustainability | Social progress which recognises the needs of everyone | Partnership working | Building long-term relationships with suppliers | Refer CIRIA report C627 *Social responsibility toolkit for construction clients* | g |
| Sustainability | Social progress which recognises the needs of everyone | Partnership working | Corporate citizenship ie resources (time/money) spent on community/socially orientated work | Refer CIRIA report C627 *Social responsibility toolkit for construction clients* | g |
| Sustainability | Social progress which recognises the needs of everyone | Partnership working | Delivering buildings and structures that provide greater satisfaction, wellbeing and value to clients and users | Refer CIRIA report C627 *Social responsibility toolkit for construction clients* | g |
| Sustainability | Social progress which recognises the needs of everyone | Partnership working | Contributing to sustainable development globally | Refer CIRIA report C627 *Social responsibility toolkit for construction clients* | g |
| Sustainability | Maintenance of high and sustainable levels of economic growth, employment and profitability | Sustained and increased productivity and profitability | Maintaining and improving profitability | Profit (before tax and interest) as a percentage of sales, profit (before tax and interest) per employee. Average normalised construction cost of a project in 2003 less the normalised cost of a similar project in 2002, expressed as a percentage of the latter. Company value added per employee (£) reported in 2003 (value added is turnover less all costs sub-contracted to, or supplied by, other parties) | g |
| Sustainability | Maintenance of high and sustainable levels of economic growth, employment and profitability | Sustained and increased productivity and profitability | Maintaining and improving productivity | The average normalised time to construct a project in 2003 less the normalised time to construct a project in 2002, expressed as a percentage of the latter | g |
| Sustainability | Maintenance of high and sustainable levels of economic growth, employment and profitability | Improved project delivery | Client satisfaction | Average client satisfaction with the finished product or facility, for projects completed in 2003, using a 1 to 10 scale | g |

| Overarching Objective | Government principles | Theme for Award Scheme Level 1 | Key issues for Award Scheme criteria Level 2 | Sub-issues for Award Scheme criteria Level 3 | Applicable to (design/construction/generic) |
|---|---|---|---|---|---|
| Sustainability | Maintenance of high and sustainable levels of economic growth, employment and profitability | Improved project delivery | Maximising quality, minimising defects | | g |
| Sustainability | Maintenance of high and sustainable levels of economic growth, employment and profitability | Improved project delivery | Maximising quality, minimising defects. Shorter, and more predictable completion time | Average actual duration at "commit to construct" less the estimated duration at "commit to invest", expressed as a percentage of the latter | g |
| | | | | Average actual duration at "available for use" less the estimated duration at "commit to construct", expressed as a percentage of the latter | g |
| Sustainability | Maintenance of high and sustainable levels of economic growth, employment and profitability | Improved project delivery | Lower cost projects with increased cost predictability | Average actual cost at "available for use" less the estimated cost at "commit to construct", expressed as a percentage of the latter | g |
| | | | | Average actual cost at "available for use" less the estimated cost at "commit to invest", expressed as a percentage of the latter | g |
| Sustainability | Maintenance of high and sustainable levels of economic growth, employment and profitability | Monitoring and reporting performance against targets | Company reporting | | g |
| Sustainability | Maintenance of high and sustainable levels of economic growth, employment and profitability | Monitoring and reporting performance against targets | Benchmarking performance | | g |
| Sustainability | Maintenance of high and sustainable levels of economic growth, employment and profitability | Designing for whole life costing (life cycle analysis) | Low maintenance and running cost, product recyclability and reuse and product life expectancy | To what degree issues associated with life cycle analysis have been incorporated into the design of the product (including 'buildability', use, demolition, and subsequent reuse, recycling and disposal) | d |
| | | | | To what degree issues associated with life cycle analysis have been incorporated into the construction of the product, additional to client specifications | c |

| Overarching Objective | Government principles | Theme for Award Scheme<br><br>Level 1 | Key issues for Award Scheme criteria<br><br>Level 2 | Sub-issues for Award Scheme criteria<br><br>Level 3 | Applicable to (design/construction/generic) |
|---|---|---|---|---|---|
| Sustainability | Cross-theme issues | Influence over competitors and other manufacturers | | | g |
| Sustainability | Cross-theme issues | Technology transfer | | | g |
| Sustainability | Cross-theme issues | Innovation | | | g |
| Sustainability | Cross-theme issues | Learning | | | g |

## AWARD SCHEME COMPONENTS AND SUGGESTED TIMEFRAMES

### First and subsequent award schemes

| First award scheme | Months | | | | | | | | | | | |
|---|---|---|---|---|---|---|---|---|---|---|---|---|
| **Award scheme component** | 1 | 2 | 3 | 4 | 5 | 6 | 7 | 8 | 9 | 10 | 11 | 12 |
| Establish business case and costs | ■ | | | | | | | | | | | |
| Development of scheme outline and approval to go ahead (internal) | ■ | | | | | | | | | | | |
| Project management | ■ | ■ | ■ | ■ | ■ | ■ | ■ | ■ | ■ | ■ | ■ | ■ |
| Determine whether to seek external sponsorship | ■ | | | | | | | | | | | |
| Development of awards criteria (through consultation) | ■ | ■ | | | | | | | | | | |
| Approval of scheme | | | ■ | | | | | | | | | |
| Select and approach judges | | | ■ | | | | | | | | | |
| Prepare promotional material for suppliers and contractors | | | ■ | | | | | | | | | |
| Scheme launch | | | ■ | | | | | | | | | |
| Promotion of the award scheme to suppliers and contractors | | | ■ | ■ | | | | | | | | |
| Preparation of submissions by suppliers and contractors | | | | ■ | ■ | | | | | | | |
| Screening award submissions | | | | | ■ | ■ | | | | | | |
| Judging panel asses award submissions* | | | | | | | ■ | | | | | |
| Prepare promotional material to highlight examples of good practice | | | | | | | ■ | ■ | | | | |
| Prepare promotional material about awards and success of scheme | | | | | | | | ■ | ■ | | | |
| Award ceremony | | | | | | | | | ■ | | | |
| Publicise winners and runners-up | | | | | | | | | ■ | ■ | | |
| Share learning | | | | | | | | | | ■ | | |
| Consider improvements for next time scheme is run (annually/biannualy) | | | | | | | | | | ■ | ■ | |

\* This could incorporate an event where brief presentations are made by all short-listed submissions).

*Time can be saved when running subsequent schemes by utilising the learning from running the first scheme.*

| Subsequent award schemes | Months | | | | | | | | | | | |
|---|---|---|---|---|---|---|---|---|---|---|---|---|
| **Award scheme component** | 1 | 2 | 3 | 4 | 5 | 6 | 7 | 8 | 9 | 10 | 11 | 12 |
| Establish business case and costs | ■ | | | | | | | | | | | |
| Development of scheme outline and approval to go ahead(internal) | ■ | ■ | ■ | ■ | ■ | ■ | | | | | | |
| Project management | ■ | | | | | | | | | | | |
| Determine whether to seek external sponsorship | ■ | | | | | | | | | | | |
| Develop of awards criteria (through consultation & based on previous scheme) | ■ | | | | | | | | | | | |
| Approval of scheme | ■ | | | | | | | | | | | |
| Select and approach judges | ■ | | | | | | | | | | | |
| Prepare promotional material for suppliers and contractors | ■ | | | | | | | | | | | |
| Scheme launch | | ■ | | | | | | | | | | |
| Promotion of the award scheme to suppliers and contractors | | ■ | ■ | | | | | | | | | |
| Preparation of submissions by suppliers and contractors | | ■ | ■ | | | | | | | | | |
| Screening award submissions | | | | ■ | | | | | | | | |
| Judging panel asses award submissions* | | | | ■ | | | | | | | | |
| Prepare promotional material to highlight examples of good practice | | | | ■ | | | | | | | | |
| Prepare promotional material about awards and success of scheme | | | | ■ | | | | | | | | |
| Award ceremony | | | | ■ | | | | | | | | |
| Publicise winners and runners-up | | | | ■ | | | | | | | | |
| Share learning | | | | | ■ | ■ | | | | | | |
| Consider improvements for next time scheme is run (annually/biannualy) | | | | | | ■ | | | | | | |

\* This could incorporate an event where brief presentations are made by all short-listed submissions).

# Appendix 2

A criteria matrices spreadsheet similar to the one shown below could be used to assess and score supplier performance.

| Level 1: The Key Themes | | Level 1 Weighting (1-3) | Performance (1-5 avoiding scores of 3) | Overall Score |
|---|---|---|---|---|
| *Effective protection of the environment and prudent use of natural resources* | | | | |
| 1 | Avoiding pollution | | | |
| 2 | Protecting and enhancing biodiversity | | | |
| 3 | Improving energy efficiency and management | | | |
| 4 | Efficient use of resources | | | |
| 5 | Transport and travel planning | | | |
| *Social progress which recognises the needs of everyone* | | | | |
| 6 | Respect for people | | | |
| 7 | Working with local communities | | | |
| 8 | Partnership working | | | |
| *Maintenance of high levels of economic growth and employment* | | | | |
| 9 | Increased productivity and profitability | | | |
| 10 | Improved project delivery | | | |
| 11 | Monitoring and reporting performance against targets | | | |
| 12 | Designing for whole life costing (life cycle analysis) | | | |
| *Cross-theme issues* | | | | |
| 13 | Influence over competitors and other manufacturers | | | |
| 14 | Technology transfer | | | |
| 15 | Innovation | | | |
| 16 | Learning | | | |
| 17 | Ethical investment regarding development of own organisation | | | |
| 18 | Ethical investment regarding other companies | | | |
| **TOTAL SCORE** | | | | |

## OUTLINE OF INDICATIVE COSTS BREAKDOWN

The table below provides an illustration of the costs of developing an award scheme for supply chain companies, based on sustainable construction. The table shows the number of days and cash costs required. A nominal internal day rate of £200 has been used to determine the total indicative costs. Where external judges are used they may requireme a payment (see Section 3.7) and a day rate of £500 may be appropriate.

Note: For timing associated with each task, see Appendix 1.

| Task | Option 1 (inexpensive) | | | | Option 1 (comprehensive) | | | | |
| --- | --- | --- | --- | --- | --- | --- | --- | --- | --- |
| | Client Project Manager | Client: Marketing | Client Project Team | Other Client Costs | Client | Client: Marketing | Client Project Team | Other Client Costs | Judges |
| Establish business case and costs | 0.5 | | | | 0.5 | | | | |
| Development of scheme outline and approval to go ahead with scheme (internal | 2.5 | | | | 1.5 | | | | |
| Project management | 11 | | | | 17 | | | | |
| Determine whether to seek external sponsorship | 0.25 | 0.25 | | | 0.25 | 0.25 | | | |
| Development of awards criteria (through consultation) | 10.5 | | | | 16.5 | | | | 1.5 |
| Approval of scheme | 0.5 | | | | 0.5 | | | | |
| Select and approach judges | 0.5 | | | | 2 | | | | |
| Prepare promotional material for suppliers & contractors | 2.5 | 1 | | | 2.5 | 5 | | £2500 | |
| Scheme launch | 1 | 0.5 | | | 2 | 5 | | £5000 | |
| Promotion of award scheme to suppliers & contractors | 4 | | 10 | | 9 | | 20 | | |
| Preparation of award submissions by suppliers & contractors | 1 | | | | 8 | | 10 | | |
| Screening award submissions | 2.5 | | | | 7 | | | | |
| Judging panel assess award submissions | 2.5 | | | | 5 | 5 | 5 | £5000 | 4.5 |
| Preparation of promotional material to highlight examples of good practice | 1.5 | | | | 3 | 10 | | £15000 + | |
| Preparation of promotional material about awards and success of scheme | 3 | 1 | | | 3 | 2.5 | | | |
| Awards ceremony | 3 | | | | 6 | 5 | 5 | £5000 | 3 |
| Prizes | | | | £0 | | | | £1500 | |
| Publicise winners and runners-up | | 1 | | | 0.5 | 3 | | £5000 | |
| Share learning | 0.5 | | | | 1.5 | 0.5 | 0.5 | | |
| Consider improvements for next time scheme is run | 0.5 | | | | 1 | 1 | 1 | | |
| | Days | | | Cash | Days | | | Cash | |
| TOTAL | 47.25 | 2.75 | 10 | 0 | 89.75 | 37.25 | 41.5 | 24 000 | 9 |
| TOTAL COSTS (days @£200 + cash costs) | £12 200 (plus cost of judges) | | | | £57 700 plus cost of judges | | | | £1500 Internal judges / £1500 External judges (if paid) |

# Appendix 4

## SUBMISSION PRO-FORMA

Below is a template pro forma that supply chain leaders may choose to use as a basis for the development of the submission form as part of their own award scheme. This has been based on the award scheme pro forma used by BAA's "Environmental Construction Awards" and Network Rail's "Annual Environment Awards".

---

### ABC Client/Main Contractors Sustainable Construction Awards 2004

This new, high profile award scheme has been developed in partnership to recognise sustainability good practice in construction by *ABC CLIENT/MAIN CONTRACTORS* and its supply chain partners. Any *ABC CLIENT/MAIN CONTRACTORS* construction project completed after *[date]* or currently at any stage in the project process can be submitted for consideration. Awards will be presented in *[date]*

The size of the project or project element is not important. What counts is the size of the contribution it makes towards achieving the highest standards of sustainability performance. The closing date for the 2004 Awards is *[date]*. A panel, which includes *ABC CLIENT/MAIN CONTRACTORS*, and independent judges, will assess the submissions and award nominees will be invited to attend the awards ceremony, which will be held in *[date]*.

For more details of the *ABC CLIENT/MAIN CONTRACTORS* Sustainable Construction Award and a nomination form contact…..

The criteria against which submissions will be appraised are focused on Environmental, Economic and Social factors and judges will be looking for submissions that demonstrate (priority areas are highlighted in bold):

| | |
|---|---|
| ○ Avoiding Pollution | ○ Designing for whole life costing (life cycle analysis) |
| ○ Protecting and enhancing biodiversity | ○ Influence over competitors and other manufacturers |
| ○ Improving energy efficiency and management | ○ Technology transfer |
| ○ Efficient use of resources | ○ Innovation |
| ○ Transport and travel planning | ○ Learning |
| ○ Respect for people | ○ Ethical investment regarding development of own organisation |
| ○ Working with local communities | ○ Ethical investment regarding other companies |
| ○ Partnership working | |
| ○ Increased productivity and profitability | |
| ○ Improved project delivery | |
| ○ Monitoring and reporting performance against targets | |

Submissions will be considered for an award in one or more of the following categories and we are therefore inviting nominations under all these headings:

- ○ projects
- ○ individual members of *ABC CLIENT/MAIN CONTRACTORS* Staff
- ○ HQ Directorates and Zones/Regions
- ○ suppliers/contractors
- ○ other

A panel, which includes *ABC CLIENT/MAIN CONTRACTORS*, and independent judges, will assess the submissions and award nominees will be invited to attend the awards ceremony, which will be held in *[date]*.

To be successful, a nomination should show a contribution against one or more of these headings. The Awards are intended to recognise individuals and organisations that have made an exceptional contribution and have gone beyond of *ABC CLIENT/MAIN CONTRACTOR'S* standard Terms and Conditions with contractors.

To make a nomination for an *ABC CLIENT/MAIN CONTRACTORS* Environmental Construction Award, simply complete the form overleaf. The closing date for the 2004 Awards is *[date]*.

---

**Title of entry** _____

**Nominated by** _____

**Organisation** _____

**Telephone No.** _____

**email address** _____

**Address** _____

_____

**Preoject summary**

Use this space to provide a 100 word summary of the nature of the submission and why you think it should be nominated for an Environmental Construction Award. Use the reverse of this page to provide more detail.

Please return the completed form to *ABC CLIENT/MAIN CONTRACTORS* by post or email
The closing date for the 2004 Awards is *[date]*.

Use this space to provide more detail about the nomination, using some or all of the following as a guide.

- Demonstrate the overall approach including options considered, key decisions and constraints.
- Make clear how the activity fulfils one or more of the award scheme criteria.
- Explain the environmental significance of the contribution made by the activity and demonstrate how it contributes to environmental quality.
- Explain how the activity achieves higher levels of environmental performance in relation to regulatory standards, *ABC CLIENT/MAIN CONTRACTORS* corporate objectives and external benchmarks.

Additional information may be submitted on separate sheets but these should be limited to 8 pages.

# Appendix 5

## CASE STUDIES

The following case studies have been produced as a result of the implementation of environmental and sustainable construction award schemes, drawing from this guidance document. Case studies of BAA, Thames Water and Network Rail are included.

## BAA Sustainable Construction Award 2001

### Establish business case and costs

In 2000 BAA developed and an Environment Award Scheme for their supply chain companies. This was well received by participants and by the wider industry, providing the winning and shortlisted submissions with recognition from BAA and amongst their peers. With this experience, the costs and business benefits of such a scheme were well understood by BAA.

BAA is widely regarded as a leading construction client. It is through initiatives such as the award schemes that this reputation is maintained and enhanced, clearly demonstrating their commitment to the environmental and sustainable performance of their supply chain.

### Determine whether to seek external sponsorship

External sponsorship was not thought to be appropriate for the award scheme as this may have diluted the message of BAA partnership with all supply chain companies.

### Development of scheme outline and aim of the scheme (including development of award categories)

BAA have a Sustainable Development Committee at group level, with members cross-cutting all aspects of BAA's activities. This committee acted as coordinator for the initial Environment Award Scheme. The possible expansion of the award scheme to sustainable construction was put onto a meeting agenda for discussion. Members of the Sustainable Development Committee considered the previous award scheme to have been a great success:

- internally – feeling that the company were acting proactively to encourage best practice
- within the supply chain – recognition given to those adopting innovative best practice
- amongst wider industry and other stakeholders – recognising BAA's stance regarding environmental issues.

The group considered that an award scheme should be run again and that the scope of the scheme should be expanded to cover sustainability. A small award scheme sub-group was established with the remit of developing the award categories and undertaking preliminary work on the awards criteria and timeframes. Membership included representatives from across BAA and also from CIRIA. This group decided that there should be just one award category, covering all aspects of sustainable construction.

### Development of award's criteria

Using this generic guide document as a basis the criteria for BAA's Sustainable Construction Award were developed as shown below. These criteria were used for both the shortlisting and judging of submissions.

| | |
|---|---|
| **1** | Does the submission describe a clear sustainable aim in line with BAA's priorities? (ie. did the team clearly set out to achieve something?) |
| | **Environment – Yes/No**  **Economic – Yes/No**  **Social – Yes/No** |
| **2** | Would the submission make a good "sharing best practice" presentation? (Yes/No) |
| **3** | Does the submission demonstrate good practice beyond minimum expected standards (please identify by scoring relevant criteria below) (Yes/No) |

| **Questions 4–19 score criteria as follows:** | | | |
|---|---|---|---|
| **1–5 (5 = Excellent note : Avoid using a score of 3)** | | | |
| **4** | Avoiding pollution | **12** | Increased productivity and profitability |
| **5** | Protecting and enhancing biodiversity | **13** | Monitoring and reporting performance against tar- |
| **6** | Improving energy efficiency and management | **14** | Designing for whole life costing (life cycle analysis) |
| **7** | Efficient use of resources | **15** | Influence over competitors and other manufactur- |
| **8** | Transport and travel planning | **16** | Technology transfer |
| **9** | Respect for people | **17** | Innovation |
| **10** | Working with local communities | **18** | Learning |
| **11** | Partnership working | **19** | Learning |

The magazine advert was included in BAA's internal magazine *In Context* and the poster campaign was used in BAA offices around the UK. A new logo and strap-line "towards a sustainable future" were also developed and utilised on promotional materials.

The criteria for the award were included in much of the promotional material, which suppliers could also view on BAA's intranet site.

### Scheme launch

The scheme was launched in late November 2001, with submissions due by mid January 2002. In the month before the launch, the award scheme was heavily promoted using the posters above and also more direct contact with supply chain companies.

### Promotion of the award scheme to supply chain companies

The scheme was open to submissions from all BAA's supply chain members involved in construction work. The primary promotional mechanism involved briefing BAA project managers on the sustainable construction award, and delivering a series of presentations to project teams. BAA project managers would then encourage their project teams to submit entries. Additionally posters and adverts were used as shown above. BAA's Intranet site was also utilised to promote the scheme to supply chain partners. The submission form was designed to be as clear and concise as possible, to encourage entries. Submissions were encouraged from the entire project team.

### Preparation of submissions by supply chain companies

Significant support was available for supply chain partners when developing submissions for the award scheme. Contact details of BAA's sustainability advisors were provided on all promotional literature. Additionally, BAA project managers could be called upon, who could then contact the sustainability advisors if suitable. Due to promotion by BAA project managers, submissions were orientated around whole projects, although specific elements of projects were also applicable.

### Screening of awards submissions

Due to the high number of award scheme submissions (17 in total), a screening process was utilised to shortlist 6 submissions. This process was undertaken by the award-scheme sub-group, consisting of representatives from BAA and CIRIA. The award scheme criteria (as shown above) was used to screen submissions. Each representative worked through each of the submissions individually, following which a meeting was held to compare, discuss and agree results.

### Judging panel assess award submissions against criteria

Judges were sent the six shortlisted submissions several weeks before the date of the award ceremony. This enabled judges to familiarise themselves with each submission.

### Preparation of promotional material to highlight examples of good practice and the success of the award scheme

A promotional leaflet was produced highlighting all award scheme submissions. Each shortlisted submission was featured on half a page, including a photo of the project or image of the planned project. This was circulated to all award ceremony attendees, in addition to further copies being distributed within BAA and supply chain companies.

### Award ceremony

The award ceremony was held on 17 April 2002 at hotel near Gatwick airport. A high quality venue was selected to encourage invitees to attend. Approximately 150 people attended, primarily consisting of representatives from BAA and supply chain companies. The format was a series of presentations from each of the shortlisted submissions to all selected supply chain attendees. Following this, judges retired to discuss and decide upon a runner up and an overall winner. A formal dinner was held in the evening which was followed by the announcement and presentations to the runners-up and the BAA Sustainable Construction Award Scheme 2001 winner by Mike Casper, deputy chief executive of BAA.

### Publicise winners and runners up

Details of all entries were summarised in a specifically developed Sustainable Construction Awards leaflet, circulated internally around BAA. Each shortlisted submission received a ½ page feature, including a photograph/picture, with a feature being made of the winner.

BAA allowed an advertising budget for the scheme, which included an eight-page promotional insert in the *New Civil Engineer* magazine *(NCE)*. This allowed the awards to be effectively publicised to the wider industry and other stakeholders, providing well-earned recognition to the winning entry, runners up and BAA.

The overall winner of the BAA Sustainable Construction Award Scheme 2001 was the Heathrow Construction Consolidation centre project team. The judges especially recognised:

- a holistic approach
- social, economic and environmetnal benefits to BAA and the local community
- innovation for the construction industry
- high transferability
- full involvement of the supply chain.

The runner up was the Glasgow car park project team, where the judges recognised:

- a fully involved supply chain
- local workforce and community involvement
- social benefits and respect for people
- environmetnal benefits through transport reductions.

Extensive publicity was also included on BAA's web and Intranet sites including all shortlisted entries, runners-up and the winner.

BAA's internal magazines, *In Context* and *Airwaves*, also featured articles on the winning submission to the award scheme.

### Share learning

Learning has been shared within BAA, building on the previous year's Environment Award Scheme, through internal promotional literature outlined above, and also by having senior BAA representatives attend the award ceremony and dinner. Externally learning has been shared with the industry and other stakeholders through selected invitations to the awards ceremony and dinner, promotion in *NCE*, and also through BAA's input to this publication.

## Thames Water

### Establish business case and costs

Thames Water had run an Engineering Award for the last eight years in various forms and therefore clearly understood the business benefits and costs associated with running such a scheme.

### Determine whether to seek external sponsorship

Thames Water decided that it was not appropriate to seek external sponsorship for their award scheme as the scheme was an initiative to work with and reward their supply chain for best practice. It was considered that external sponsorship may dilute this message.

### Development of scheme outline and aim of the scheme (including development of award categories)

Within the Thames Water Engineering Awards 2002 there were seven categories, of which sustainable construction was one:

- Meeting customer needs
- Partners and suppliers
- Sustainable construction
- Innovation and creativity
- Outperforming the capital programme
- Enabling profitable growth
- Developing our people.

### Development of awards criteria

Within the sustainable construction category, the judging criteria were developed by a sustainable construction working party consisting of members from CIRIA and Thames Water. Criteria were developed drawing on this guidance document and specifically covered:

- avoiding pollution
- protecting and enhancing biodiversity
- improving energy efficiency and management
- efficient use of resources
- transport and travel planning
- designing for whole life costing
- monitoring and reporting performance against targets.

### Approval of scheme

The award scheme has been approved and supported by senior management. The inclusion of a sustainable construction category further supports the commitment to continual improvement that Thames Water have made through their environmental management system accreditation to ISO14001.

### Select and approach judges

Thames Water decided that the judging panel should consist of representatives from within Thames Water and other stakeholders, including from their supply chain and construction research organisations. A team of seven judges was selected, with each judge having overall responsibility for one of the Engineering Award Scheme categories (shown above).

### Prepare promotional material for suppliers and contractors

The posters below were prepared to promote the award scheme to Thames Water's current and previous suppliers and contractors.

### Scheme launch

The scheme was launched to the integrated teams of design, construction and supply through a poster campaign in the engineering office and the offices of the alliance teams. Further promotion was carried out using the Thames Water intranet; accessed by the integrated teams. Regular reminders about the award scheme were posted as notices on the intranet and, finally, presentations were made about the scheme in each of the offices.

### Promotion of the award scheme to suppliers/partners

Thames Water decided on a multi-faceted approach when promoting the scheme to suppliers, contractors and partners. Firstly, the scheme was promoted through the posters shown above. These were displayed in high profile locations at Thames Water offices. Secondly, the Thames Water intranet heavily promoted the scheme, providing further information of the benefits and how to enter. Thirdly, all Thames Water engineering teams and project managers were briefed well in advance of the scheme launch using the engineering cascade system, which focuses on a series of monthly meetings. In addition the internal monthly newsletter was used to promote the Engineering Award Scheme. Submissions were encouraged from the entire project team.

### Preparation of submissions by supply chain companies

Submissions were requested in paper and electronic format to any one of the nine award categories. The same submission was not allowed to be entered in more than one category. A total of 43 submissions were received across the nine award categories. Four submissions were received in the sustainable construction category, each of which was of a very high standard.

### Screening of awards submissions

In each category there was a small working group that determined a shortlist from the award scheme submissions. In the sustainable construction category, using the criteria, the sustainable construction working party determined that from the four submissions in this category, two should be shortlisted:

- Terra Eco and the Trident West Alliance – Little Marlow composting
- Reading target team – Reading sewage treatment plant.

### Judging panel assess award submissions against criteria

Judging was undertaken on 19 June 2002 at Thames Water offices, Reading. All shortlisted submissions were asked to prepare and deliver a 10-minute presentation in support of their submission. Following this the judges compared criteria judging sheets and agreed a winner and runner-up for each category.

### Preparation of promotional material to highlight examples of good practice

Photos and details of the winning entry and runner-up in each category were highlighted on the Thames Water intranet. Additionally posters were produced which were displayed in high profile locations around the Thames Water offices.

### Preparation of promotional material about awards and success of scheme

Thames Water assisted CIRIA in the development of this report to highlight the success of their award scheme. Additionally, Thames Water use the award scheme initiative to support tenders as proof of their efforts and commitment to encouraging best practice working within their supply chain.

### Award ceremony

The award ceremony was held on 19 June 2002, at the Berkshire Brewery, Reading, chosen for its proximity to Thames Water offices. All team members from shortlisted submissions were invited. Each judge for the seven categories then announced the winner and runner up for their category. The winner in the Thames Water Engineering Awards 2002 Sustainable Construction category was the Reading Target team for the design, construction and commissioning of the new Reading sewage treatment works. The runner up was Terra Eco and the Trident West Alliance for the sustainable solution to Little Marlow composting.

### Publicise winners and runners up

Winners were publicised via the Thames Water intranet and through the use of posters displayed in high profile locations around the Thames Water offices.

### Share learning

Almost all of the 43 submissions to the Thames Water Engineering Awards 2002 were relevant to at least one element of sustainable construction. Companies making entries may, therefore, have been undecided as to which category to submit their entry. Although in the 2002 awards, the sustainable construction criteria was focused primarily on the environmental area of sustainability, which could be expanded upon in future years.

# Network Rail Environment Awards for 2002

**Establish business case and costs**

For three preceding years, Network Rail had, under their previous name of Railtrack, run their annual Environment Awards. The costs and business benefits, such as partnership working and encouraging best practice innovation, were well recognised.

**Determine whether to seek external sponsorship**

External sponsorship was not thought to be appropriate for these awards. Network Rail wanted the awards to be seen as their own initiative to provide recognition of best practice.

**Development of scheme outline and aim of the scheme (including development of award categories)**

Network Rail's intention was to recognise individuals and organisations that had made an exceptional contribution to environmental performance, going beyond what would normally be expected from an individual or project.

**Development of awards criteria**

Following the tradition of the Chairman's Environment Awards, and due to the diverse nature of potential award nominations, Network Rail decided to offer a suite of awards in the following categories:

- Individual members of staff
- HQ Directorates
- Railtrack Zones/Regions
- Large Contractors/Alliances
- Small to medium contractors
- Train/Freight operating companies
- Major Projects
- Best Station (new category)
- Suppliers (new category).

The awards criteria were developed by Network Rail and CIRIA based on this guide, focusing on environmental criteria:

- effective environmental protection
- enhancement and protection of biodiversity and heritage
- efficient use of resources and energy
- sustainable and integrated transport systems
- improvements in environmental management systems
- building partnerships with key stakeholders.

Cross cutting themes, (considered within each of the above criteria)

- innovation
- transferability and learning.

**Approval of scheme**

The scheme, as outlined above, was approved internally by Network Rail's environmental team.

**Select and approach judges**

It was decided that award scheme judges should remain consistent with the previous Chairman's Environment Awards. This consisted of high level representatives from Network Rail in addition to a representative from the sustainability think-tank Forum for the Future. Judges were selected to highlight the importance Network Rail gave to the awards, and further credibility was added through the appointment of an external representative.

### Prepare promotional material for suppliers and contractors

Network Rail prepared simple guidelines for individuals/companies considering submitting entries to the awards. The guidance firstly had a quote from Network Rail's chief executive, highlighting Network Rail's commitment to the awards. Then followed an introduction to the rail industry and the environment, before details of the forthcoming award ceremony, categories and criteria were provided.

For the individual award, nominations were requested. Other categories, ie contractors, suppliers, train/freight operating companies, zones/regions, HQ directorates, major projects and stations, were invited to submit an application on their own behalf. Further information was then provided on the criteria, giving a guide of how each of the criteria could be fulfilled.

### Scheme launch

The scheme was launched in September 2002 with submissions due by mid-November 2002. Guidance was provided to participants regarding:

- scheme categories
- scheme criteria
- entry requirements

Additional telephone support was also available.

### Promotion of the award scheme to suppliers/partners

The importance of the award was highlighted to suppliers/partners using a quote from Network Rail's chairman, John Armitt, who stated that the Annual Network Rail Environment Awards were: "A celebration of the achievement of the whole rail industry in continuously improving environmental performance." An introduction to environmental management and the rail industry was then provided, followed by greater detail regarding the award scheme.

Network Rail were keen to ensure that it was very easy to make a nomination for the awards. Therefore a clear and concise one-page form was developed, which is shown opposite. Any supporting information could also be provided with the form. Submissions were requested electronically, by email

### Preparation of submissions

Support was available for individuals/ companies submitting entries to the awards via telephone and e-mail. Contact details of Network Rail's award scheme co-ordinator were provided on the award scheme guidance.

### Screening of awards submissions

Award submissions in construction orientated categories were screened through discussions between Network Rail and CIRIA. These categories were:

- HQ Directorates
- Large Contractors/Alliances
- Small to medium contractors
- Major Projects
- Suppliers

Up to three or four submissions were shortlisted in each category.

# THE ANNUAL NETWORK RAIL ENVIRONMENT AWARDS 2002

## Entry form

---

**NOMINATION CATEGORY**
*(Tick appropriate box)*

| | | | | | |
|---|---|---|---|---|---|
| Individual | ☐ | Directorate – HQ | ☐ | Zone/Region | ☐ |
| Small/Medium Contractor | ☐ | Large Contractor | ☐ | Train/Freight Operator | ☐ |
| Major Project | ☐ | Supplier | ☐ | Station | ☐ |

**NOMINEE DETAILS**
*(Complete relevant section)*

**NETWORK RAIL INDIVIDUAL: Surname** _____  **Forename** _____

**NETWORK RAIL BUSINESS UNIT: Region/Directorate** _____ **Director** _____

**COMPANY (eg Contractor)** _____ **Director** _____

**ADDRESS** _____

_____

_____

**TEL** _____  **EMAIL** _____

**JUDGING AREAS COVERED**
*(Tick those areas you feel your submission covers)*

☐ 1 Effective environmental protection
☐ 2 Enhancement and protection of biodiversity and heritage
☐ 3 Efficient use of resources and energy
☐ 4 Sustainable and integrated transport systems
☐ 5 Improvements in environmental management systems
☐ 6 Building partnerships with key stakeholders

**DETAILS OF NOMINATOR**
*(Please provide your contact details in case further information is required & please sign the form)*

**SURNAME** _____  **FORENAME** _____

**ADDRESS** _____

**TEL** _____  **EMAIL** _____

**SIGNATURE** _____  **DATE** _____

**DETAILS OF VERIFYING MANAGER**
*(Please provide a contact who can verify that the submission is accurate)*

**SURNAME** _____  **FORENAME** _____

**ADDRESS** _____

**TEL** _____  **EMAIL** _____

Please return by email to mcmurtriel.railtrack@ems.rail.co.uk by the 15th November 2002

---

### Judging panel assess award submissions against criteria

The judging panel consisted of high-level management representatives from Network Rail, including John Armitt, the Network Rail Chief Executive, and externally from the sustainability think-tank Forum for the Future. Judges were selected based on their knowledge of the rail industry and environmental issues. Judges had already been involved in the previous Railtrack Environment Awards, and they used the award criteria developed by Network Rail, which was based on this guidance document.

### Preparation of promotional material to highlight the success of the scheme and examples of good practice

Following the judging of the award submissions, Network Rail developed a promotional leaflet outlining briefly the purpose of the Environment Awards 2002, and providing a summary of each of the winning entries. This was not released until after the award ceremony.

### Award ceremony

The Network Rail Environment Awards 2002 ceremony was held at the Tate Britain on the evening of 4th March 2003. Approximately 160 delegates attended, including representatives from all shortlisted, other supply chain partners, key stakeholders and Network Rail employees. The format of the event was a wine reception and formal dinner, followed by the announcement and presentations to the winners in each of the nine award categories by John Armitt.

### Publicise winners and runners up

Following the award ceremony the winning entries were publicised in a joint Network Rail/*New Civil Engineer* report. The four-page report was included in the March edition of *NCE*. Each winning entry received a half-page summary, with shortlisted submissions also mentioned.

The winning entries to the Network Rail Environment Awards 2002 are as follows:

- ○ Individual members of Railtrack Staff — Toby Meadows, Network Rail Eastern Region
- ○ HQ Directorates — Major Stations
- ○ Railtrack Zones/Regions — Eastern Region
- ○ Large Contractors/Alliances — West Anglia Route Modernisation
- ○ Small to medium contractors — Avondale Environmental Services
  Special mention – Bittern Line Partnership
- ○ Train/Freight operating companies — Thameslink
- ○ Major Projects — Carillion Rail
- ○ Best Station (new category) — Piccadilly, Manchester
- ○ Suppliers (new category) — Holdfast Level Crossings

### Share learning

Learning has been shared within Network Rail, building on previous environment award schemes. Externally learning has been shared with the industry and other stakeholders through the awards ceremony, promotion in *NCE*, and also through Network Rail's input to this publication.

# Appendix 6

## SUPPORTING GUIDANCE

| | Further information available from: |
|---|---|
| ○ Sustainable construction: company indicators (C563) | **CIRIA**<br>www.ciria.org |
| ○ Sustainable Construction Pioneers Club (Research Project 644) | **CIRIA**<br>www.ciria.org |
| ○ A Guide to good practice: Organising & Sponsoring Environment and Sustainable Development Awards | **Royal Society for the encouragement of Arts, Manufacture and Commerce (RSA)**<br>www.EnvironmentAwards.net |
| ○ B&Q QUEST for suppliers | **B&Q**<br>www.diy.co.uk |
| ○ BAA Environmental Award Scheme | **BAA**<br>www.baa.com |
| ○ Network Rail Chairman's Annual Environmental Awards | **Network Rail**<br>www.networkrail.co.uk |

# Appendix 7

## LINKS TO KEY ORGANISATIONS

### Project Steering Group members

| | |
|---|---|
| **B&Q** | Tel: 02380 256256<br>Web: www.diy.com |
| **BAA plc** | Tel: 020 7834 9449<br>Web: www.baa.com |
| **CIRIA** | Tel: 020 7549 3300<br>Web: www.ciria.org |
| **Highways Agency** | Tel: 08459 556 575<br>Web: www,highways.gov.uk |
| **Housing Corporation** | Tel: 020 7393 2000<br>Web: www.housingcorp.gov.uk |
| **Rail Link Engineering** | Tel: 020 7681 5000<br>Web: www.ctrl.co.uk |
| **Royal Society for the encouragement of Arts, Manufactures and Commerce (RSA)** | Tel: 020 7930 5115<br>Web: www.rsa.org.uk |
| **Thames Water** | Tel: 0845 9200 800<br>Web: www.thameswater.co.uk |
| **Royal Bank of Scotland** | Tel: 0131 523 7400<br>Web: www.rbs.co.uk |
| **Network Rail** | Tel: 020 7557 8000<br>Web: www.networkrail.co.uk |
| **The Housing Corporation** | Tel: 020 7393 2000<br>Web: www.housingcorp.gov.uk |

### Other useful organisations

| | |
|---|---|
| **Association of Certified Chartered Accountants** | Tel: 0141 582 2222<br>Web: wwwacca.co.uk |
| **The BOC Foundation** | Tel: 01403 820021<br>Web: www.boc.com/foundation |
| **Building Research Establishment** | Tel: 01923 664000<br>Web: www.bre.co.uk |
| **Business in the Community** | Tel: 0870 600 2482<br>Web: www.bitc.org.uk |
| **Campaign to Protect Rural England** | Tel: 020 7981 2800<br>Web: www.cpre.org.uk |
| **Construction Federation** | Tel: 020 7608 5000<br>Web: www.thecc.org.uk |

| **Department of Trade and Industry (DTI)** | Tel: 020 7215 5000<br>Web: www.dti.gov.uk | |
| --- | --- | --- |
| **Department for Environment Food and Rural Affairs (DEFRA)** | Tel: 08459 33 55 77<br>Web: www.defra.gov.uk | |
| **Forum for the Future** | Tel: 020 7251 6070<br>Web: www.forumforthefuture.org.uk | |
| **Environment Agency National Headquarters** | Tel: 01454 624 400<br>Web: www.environment-agency.gov.uk | |
| **Environment Agency Regional offices** | **Anglian**<br>Tel: 01733 371811 | **Southern**<br>Tel: 01903 832000 |
| | **Midlands**<br>Tel: 0121 711 2324 | **South West**<br>Tel: 01392 444 000 |
| | **North East**<br>Tel: 0113 244 0191 | **Thames**<br>Tel: 0118 953 5000 |
| | **North West**<br>Tel: 01925 653 999 | **Welsh**<br>Tel: 029 207 70088 |
| **Friends of the Earth** | Tel: 020 7490 1555<br>Web: www.foe.co.uk | |
| **Local Government Offices:** | **Government Office for the West Midlands**<br>Tel: 0121 212 5050<br>Web: www.go-wm.gov.uk | **Government office for the North West**<br>Tel: 0161 952 4000<br>Web: www.go-nw.gov.uk |
| | **Government office for the East of England**<br>Tel: 01223 372500<br>Web: www.go-east.gov.uk | **Government Office for the South East**<br>Tel: 01483 882255<br>Web: www.go- se.gov.uk |
| | **Government Office for the East Midlands**<br>Tel: 0115 971 9971<br>Web: www.go-em.gov.uk | **Government Office for the South West**<br>Tel: 0117 900 1700<br>Web: www.gosw.gov.uk |
| | **Government Office for London**<br>Tel: 020 7217 3328<br>Web: www.go-london.gov.uk | **Government Office for Yorkshire and the Humber**<br>Tel: 0113 280 0600<br>Web: www.goyh.gov.uk |
| | **Government Office for the North East**<br>Tel: 0191 201 8100<br>Web: www.go-ne.gov.uk | |
| **Greenpeace** | Tel: 020 7865 8100<br>Web: www.greenpeace.org.uk | |
| **Movement for Innovation** | Tel: 01923 664820<br>Web: www.M4i.org.uk | |

**Regional Development Agencies**

**Advantage West Midlands**
Tel: 0121 380 3500
Web: wmda.org.uk

**East of England Development Agency**
Tel: 01223 713900
Web: www.eeda.org.uk

**East Midlands Development Agency**
Tel: 0115 988 8300
Web: www.emda.org.uk

**London Development Agency**
Tel: 020 7680 2000
Web: www.ida.gov.uk

**North West Development Agency**
Tel: 01925 400100
Tel: nwda.co.uk

**South East of England Development Agency**
Tel: 01483 484 200
Web: www.seeda.co.uk

**South West of England Development Agency**
Tel: 01392 214 747
Web: www.southwestrda.org.uk

**One North East**
Tel: 0191 229 6200
Web: www.onenortheast.co.uk

**Yorkshire Forward**
Tel: 0113 394 9600
Web: www.yorkshire-forward.com

**World Wildlife Foundation**

Tel: 01483 426444
Web: www.wwf.org.uk